FORWARD IN HEELS

Forward in Heels

by Jenny Maenpaa, LCSW, ACC, EdM

© 2018

Sections and Chapters

Introduction 1

Authenticity 5

Chapter 1: How I Got Here and How You Can
Follow My Lead 7

Chapter 2: Unleashing Your Own Personal
Leadership Vision and Making It a Reality 11

Chapter 3: Why It's Urgent and You Must Do
This NOW 23

Passion 31

Chapter 4: Your Personal Mission Statement 33

Chapter 5: What's Your Vision? 37

Chapter 6: Having it All 43

Potential 47

Chapter 7: Getting in the Right Mindset to Kick Ass 49

Chapter 8: Setting SMART Goals 55

Chapter 9: What Every Job Must Have (No Matter
How Old You Are, How Senior the Job, or What
Industry You're In) 59

Results 65

Chapter 10: Creating Your Action Plan 67

Chapter 11: Negotiating – Because You're Worth It! 69

Chapter 12: Burnout Prevention Plan...................... 75

Boldness **81**

    Chapter 13: Tying it All Together 83

    Chapter 14: Big Life Plan 87

    Chapter 15: Conclusion...91

Appendix..**95**

Introduction

Forward in Heels is a step-by-step guide to having it all for badass women who want to excel at what they do, stand tall, and own their worth so they can light up the world.

A licensed therapist and certified leadership coach shows you the secrets to unleashing your ultimate potential in all aspects of your life.

Do you feel a disconnect between your values and your work? Do you struggle with finding a career that brings you joy? Do you wonder how to derive meaning from your job while still fulfilling other areas of your life? This book will help you uncover what makes you come alive! You will learn how to tap into your own emotional intelligence to get what you want out of your work and your life by exploring your core values. When you can take care of yourself personally, your light shines through, and the best version of your professional self will manifest.

Read on if you...

- Feel a disconnect between your values and your work.

- Struggle with finding a career that brings you joy.

- Wonder how to derive meaning from your job while still fulfilling other areas of your life.

- Are not deeply unhappy, just unfulfilled. You're not miserable, you just feel some thing(s) could be better and aren't sure how to make them happen.

- Lack work/life balance and feel totally lopsided - strong in some areas and a mess in others.

This book is for any woman who is ready to make bold, lasting changes in her life. Women used to think they had to emulate men to achieve the same positions of power. Now we are realizing that unleashing our own unique, special qualities that set us apart from male leaders is how we will achieve our dreams. We are no longer dancing backwards, trying to mirror men. We are moving forward...in heels.

Frank and Ernest used with the permission of the Thaves and the Cartoonist Group. All rights reserved.[1]

Women CAN have it all when we are intentional, know our own value systems, and define what "all" means for ourselves. Once you can define it, you can figure out how to get and maintain it. "All" is not what others say it is. Figure out what your "all" is.

I only figured out my version of "having it all" once I started living according to my core values. Once you complete the activities in this book, you will know your core values, as well, and you will be able to define "having it all" for yourself and on your own terms.

This book is framed according to my 5 Core Values:

1. Authenticity - Life is not about fitting into a mold. It is about being our genuine selves and finding the space where that version of us fits perfectly.

2. Boldness - The world does not benefit from us playing it safe. We don't move mountains by staying in our comfort zones.

3. Passion - We owe it to ourselves and the world to find what makes us come alive with joy and excitement. Passion is contagious.

4. Potential - Once we find our passions, we can shine brightly and light the torches of those around us.

5. Results - Kick ass. Never apologize for being who you are, believing you deserve the best, and going after what you want.

Authenticity

Chapter 1:
How I Got Here and How You Can Follow My Lead

I began my career in social services, working with families and children in crisis. My clients were domestic violence survivors, children struggling to overcome being behind in school academically, socially, and emotionally, and adolescents involved in juvenile justice. I have met people on the worst days of their lives, the morning after their partner attacked them violently, on the day they received an autism spectrum diagnosis for their toddler, or on the day they were locked up and taken from their family for months. I loved the work I did; I got to actually see people benefit daily. I saw them able to make changes in their own lives that allowed them to never need to see me again. But I kept encountering major structural barriers to success.

In one particular position about a decade into my career, the violence between clients, community members, and staff had escalated to weekly incidents. I began experiencing trauma symptoms myself due to a combination of this community violence and toxic leadership. I was waking up in the middle of the night in a cold sweat, clenching my jaw in my sleep, physically hunching all day at work, jumping when someone approached me, and always standing with my back against a wall. Instead of addressing the systemic causes of conflict in our community, leaders were quick to blame and short on solutions. In addition, the leaders I was working under each had competing visions for our organization, which led to divergent expectations for employees.

After so many years of working in similarly high-stress environments with frequent crises, I was burning out. According to Sherrie Bourg Carter in <u>Psychology Today</u>[2], "burnout is a state of chronic stress that leads to physical and emotional exhaustion, cynicism and detachment, and feelings of ineffectiveness and lack of accomplishment." These can lead to permanent withdrawal from your work or from your personal life. Burnout, if left unchecked, can lead to myriad health problems, including fatigue, insomnia, forgetfulness, illness, anxiety, depression, anger, detachment, isolation, and hopelessness.

I met with a professional mentor and spilled all of my feelings to him, all of which were primarily rooted in fear, guilt, and anxiety. When I had finished explaining how disillusioned, rudderless, and confused I was, he asked me a question. He said, "All I keep hearing is what everyone needs from you. When will your needs be as important or more important than everyone else's?" I had no answer to that question because as a social worker, I had never given myself space to ask. He followed up by saying, "You keep talking about how you can't abandon this organization's mission. But what about *your* mission? If you stay here, you will burn out and leave the helping profession entirely, which would be a betrayal of your own personal mission." I had never heard of a personal mission before. I thought a mission statement was reserved for big companies with shareholders and a board of directors. I left this meeting with a lot to think about.

On the heels of these revelations, I spoke with a colleague within my same struggling organization. She said, "Have you ever thought about coaching?" I replied, "What like, some guru telling me to drink green juice?" She rolled her eyes. "No, like helping people become better versions of themselves via a modality that isn't therapy. You need a break right now to figure out how to keep doing the work you love in a way you can sustain. Look at the work you've done with the staff here; maybe it's time you thought about doing more work with adults that isn't crisis-focused."

With a new goal in mind, I set out to learn everything I could. I learned was that as a therapist, coaching could become one more tool in my toolbox for clients, along with my already-established strengths in cognitive behavioral therapy and motivational interviewing. So, I took the leap, enrolled in a coaching certification program, and started my own business. It was the scariest thing I've ever done, and I've made a lot of mistakes along the way. But no matter what stressors I faced, like unsteady income month-to-month, discomfort with the sales pitch aspect of gaining new clients, or fear that I was not good enough to solve everyone's problems, I wake up every day excited to work. This is because after a lifetime of trying to meet everyone else's expectations, I finally got clarity on my own expectations for myself. I unearthed my own value system (Chapter 2), created a personal mission statement (Chapter 4), and got to work putting it all into action (Chapter 10). I learned that I could write my own destiny by combining therapy with coaching to create an entirely new hybrid model for the uncharted territory we are in as women in 2018 and beyond.

I wrote this book for any woman who is struggling to find joy and meaning in her career, who feels a disconnect between her personal and professional identities, or who is trying to find that elusive work/life balance in a world that demands so much of her. So often, we are looking for someone else's permission to want what we want. Learn from my journey. Every new challenge in your life requires a stronger version of you than before. If you're not scared, you're not dreaming big enough. I figured it out and you can, too.

Chapter 2:
Unleashing Your Own Personal Leadership Vision and Making It a Reality

The first step I needed to take on my leadership journey was to figure out what I valued. In the introduction, I explained that I only figured out what my version of "having it all" is once I started living according to my core values. I finally stopped giving away my power and took control of my own story. I learned that I am not only allowed to put myself first, but in fact obligated to. Putting everyone else first will only drive you to an early grave after a life of discontent.

I now know that when I live my life in accordance with my values of authenticity, boldness, passion, potential, and results, I am following my own true north star. As long as all of my decisions come from those starting points, I will continue to maintain my own version of having it all. Happiness will always ebb and flow, but because there is no disconnect for me between my value system and my actions, I am able to have faith that a flow will always follow an ebb because I am always doing what is right for me.

Start with the activity here to figure out your own core value system. Remember that this is a safe space that no one else ever has to read and try to refrain from judging yourself.

Forward in Heels

Accomplishment
Ambition
Authenticity
Achievement
Adventure
Authority
Autonomy
Balance
Beauty
Boldness
Caring
Compassion
Challenge
Change
Citizenship
Collaboration
Comfort
Commitment
Community
Competency
Competition
Complexity
Contribution
Creativity
Curiosity
Dedication
Determination
Devotion
Discipline
Diversity
Drive
Empathy
Empowerment
Equality
Excitement
Fairness
Faith
Fame
Family

Forgiveness
Friendships
Fun
Generosity
Gratitude
Grit
Growth
Happiness
Harmony
Honesty
Honor
Humility
Humor
Idealism
Improvement
Independence
Individuality
Influence
Inspiration
Integrity
Intelligence
Joy
Justice
Kindness
Knowledge
Leadership
Learning
Love
Loyalty
Meaning
Openness
Opportunity
Optimism
Passion
Patriotism
Peace
Perfection
Perseverance
Pleasure

Poise
Popularity
Potential
Power
Prestige
Progress
Prosperity
Purpose
Reason
Recognition
Relationships
Reliability
Religion
Reputation
Resilience
Resourcefulness
Respect
Responsibility
Results
Safety
Security
Self-Reliance
Self-Respect
Sensitivity
Service
Simplicity
Spirituality
Stability
Success
Support
Status
Tolerance
Tradition
Trustworthiness
Vulnerability
Wealth
Wisdom
Zeal

Skim this list of values. It is by no means exhaustive; it is merely a place to start. Start by circling *all* of the values that matter to you personally, even if that's almost the whole list. Add any that are not listed.

Don't ascribe judgments to any values - no value is good or bad, and they can all show up in a variety of ways. It's okay if some overlap or seem redundant, and it's okay if some seem to be in conflict. We are complex beings. For example, if you are the executive director of a large social services organization, you may value social justice *as well as* status. One does not diminish the other. Because you value status, you have chosen to become the executive director so that you can have the broadest reach for the highest number of clients possible, but it does not diminish your commitment to social justice. Your work is no more or less valuable than the person doing direct work with clients, and you don't value social justice any less.

Pause here and check in with yourself. What feelings have come up? Insights? Revelations? Judgments? Anxieties? Discomfort? Resistance? Stay present with those feelings as you continue. Record those here:

_____

_____

_____

_____

Now imagine you have packed all of these values into a suitcase for the journey of your life. This suitcase is overflowing and going to be very challenging to lug with you over the hills and valleys. In order to navigate this journey, you will have to get rid of some excess values to lighten your load.

Take a few minutes and cross off at least 10 values from your list. These are still important values to you, but you may not feel that you need to focus on living according to them every day.

Now you're continuing on in your life's journey and you're feeling lighter and more purposeful. You're doing an amazing job navigating all of the unexpected challenges. However, by this point in your journey, you've been traveling for a while and there's still simply too much baggage to feel like you're really able to gain clarity.

At this juncture, cross off at least 10 more values. You're getting much lighter and clarifying your purpose more every day, but over time, you find that you are still dragging a little.

Now, as your final step toward understanding your true self, cross off the rest of the values on this list until you are down to only 10. This will be very difficult, as these values all inform who you are as a person in some way or in some circumstances. But not all of them are your true core essence.

Now think carefully about what values are central to who you are and which ones you could absolutely not get rid of. What you are feeling now?

_____

_____

_____

You're in the home stretch! One final time, whittle down your list. Choose 3-5 values and list them here:

1. _____

2. _____

3. _____

4. _____

5. _____

Think about a time when each one was especially relevant for you. These values are the most fundamental essence of who you are. These values inform everything you do, think, believe, and feel. This does not mean that you do not embody other values or that different ideas can't be important to you, as well. Rather, these are simply the umbrellas under which everything else falls. Reflect here on specific examples of when these values informed your actions.

_____

_____

_____

Reflect on the following questions:

Why did you choose these values?

_____

_____

_____

What life experiences have made each of them a core value for you?

_____

_____

_____

Are any of these values in conflict with one another?

_____

_____

_____

What did you notice about what you value most about yourself?

_____

_____

What was easy? What was difficult? What was surprising?

_____

_____

_____

Professional:

Do the majority of decisions you make at work reflect your values?

_____

_____

_____

Does your boss, manager, colleague, or anyone else with whom you work regularly value different ideas? Does this create synergy or conflict for you at work?

_____

_____

_____

Are you spending time at work chasing values that are less important to you?

_____

_____

_____

What do you wish you could spend your time pursuing at work?

_____

_____

_____

What prevents you from doing that?

_____

_____

_____

How could your life look different if this were the focus of your professional life?

_____

_____

_____

If there are mismatches between your values and how you spend your time, what is preventing you from realizing your values in action? What can you change? Remember that sometimes it's not about changing something external but changing your internal perspective and expectations.

_____

_____

_____

Finally, if what you want doesn't exist, can you create it?

_____

_____

_____

Personal:

Do the majority of decisions you make at home reflect your values?

_____

_____

_____

Does your spending reflect your values? Do the last 3 months' worth of your financial statements support this answer?

_____

_____

_____

Does your partner value different ideas? Does this create synergy or conflict for you at home?

_____

_____

_____

Are you spending time at home chasing values that are less important to you?

_____

_____

_____

What do you wish you could spend your time pursuing at home?

_____

_____

What prevents you from doing that?

How could your life look different if this were the focus of your personal life?

If there are mismatches between your values and how you spend your time, what is preventing you from realizing your values in action? What can you change? Remember that sometimes it's not about changing something external but changing your internal perspective and expectations.

Finally, if what you want doesn't exist, can you create it?

_____

_____

_____

Chapter 3:
Why It's Urgent and You Must Do This NOW

Congratulations on completing your values exercise! For most people, the values exercise is the hardest part and the place where they abandon their journey of self-discovery. This is because it asks you to be raw and vulnerable, which is a terrifying experience for most of us. Pat yourself on the back for completing the part most people quit during! You may ask, "Why does it matter that I figure all this out now? I have plenty of time and right now I need to focus on my immediate needs." While you should absolutely attend to your immediate needs, you don't need to look at your priorities as either/or. Rather, you can assign different levels of priority to your to-do list items.

In generations past, people worked hard until they retired and could then experience their lives. They traveled, took up new hobbies, and enjoyed being grandparents. However, that world no longer exists. Companies lay off employees before they reach retirement age, forcing them to work long beyond their expectations. Anyone who survived the Great Recession of 2007-2012 is still feeling its effects. Guaranteed job security is a thing of the past and the way you approach the working world needs to reflect that. In addition, millennials have come into the workforce believing that they deserve to be happy at work, which is not an idea previous generations even entertained. This idea is not limited to millennials, either, as it is spreading to workers of older generations who still have decades in their professions ahead of them.

Psychologist <u>Abraham Maslow</u>[3] created a hierarchy of needs to describe human's rational movement toward self-fulfillment and optimal functioning. Few people truly reach self-actualization but many spend their lifetimes seeking it. The outdated idea of self-actualization implies that one could ever reach a state of achieving one's full potential and remain there permanently, forever happy and content. That idea creates a false expectation that can make us feel like failures if we do not feel blissfully happy every day or even every moment. Instead, we should consider happiness as an emotion that ebbs and flows, like hunger. No matter how many times we eat, we will eventually become hungry again. Similarly, no matter how many times we achieve moments of happiness through our actions and thought processes, we will lose that feeling of happiness again at some point. The goal is to be able to regularly come back to the things that make us happy and create overall consistency in our lives, not daily perfection.

In the past, employment was expected to fulfill the bottom two sections of Maslow's Hierarchy - basic physiological needs and some measure of financial security. If you could also make friends at work and fulfill the next level, that was just an added bonus. Receiving praise and fulfilling one's potential were not standard expectations from anyone's job. Today, the working world looks different. According to Jan Tegze[4], senior recruiting manager, main reasons for employee attrition have evolved over the years. "Before 2008, a higher salary was the main motivation. After 2011, the main reasons started shifting toward things like benefits and the environment. From 2014 and on, more people started leaving their jobs for better job opportunities that provided advancements, a more supportive culture, and where managers gave them more responsibility to decide things for themselves than their current managers did (less sense of ownership)."

Praise and genuine recognition of accomplishments keep employees at a company far longer than pay raises and increased benefits. Researchers Patrick Hill and Nicholas Turiano[5] found in the Journal of Research in Personality that "since purpose is linked with greater engagement in day-to-day life, its role in financial success 'may result from the greater capability and propensity for purposeful individuals to pursue their long-term goals, which in turn promotes the accrual of assets.' Put another way: Purpose is at the intersection of hope and grit."

If we have this information and know what to pursue to achieve fulfillment, then what's the problem? The problem is that bully inside your head telling you that you are not *enough*. Not smart enough, pretty enough, ambitious enough, likable enough, thin enough, funny enough, clever enough... the list is endless. She tells you that if you could just meet those standards of perfection, everything else would fall into place. Too often, we fall into the trap of thinking, "Once _____ is perfect, then I can have what I want." Life is not an endless report card and seeking excellence is not the same as pursuing perfection. *Perfectionism is paralyzing; excellence is energizing.* It's time you took control of that toxic relationship with your bully. You are going to stand up to that mean girl in your head and put her in her place. But first, you have to know which type of mean girl she is, so that you can know exactly how to fight her.

The following quiz will help you uncover which archetype you fall into and how you are letting those nasty voices undermine you. For every archetype, there are positive and negative aspects. No one type is completely good or bad. Understanding your limitations is not about changing yourself, but about realizing that your strengths are mighty and your weaknesses are manageable. Too many quizzes and books make it complicated. It's not. Your mean girl falls into one of these simple categories and the sooner you know that, the sooner you can determine how to counteract your self-sabotaging behavior.

What Kind of Mean Girl is Sabotaging You?

For each question, circle which response most closely reflects how you feel. When you calculate your scores at the end, pay attention to how strongly you identified with a statement and mark the corresponding numbers to obtain your results.

(1) Strongly Disagree   (2) Disagree   (3) Agree
(4) Strongly Agree

1. When something needs to be done, it's easier to do it myself.

2. I often procrastinate until the last minute.

3. I am very competitive.

4. When someone makes an error, I feel a compulsive need to correct them.

5. It is important that people see me as friendly and helpful.

6. I like to work when the mood strikes me, not on a prescribed schedule.

7. It bothers me when I think someone dislikes me.

8. I need a lot of structure to work best.

9. It matters to me to know if people are pleased with my work.

10. I have trouble admitting when I am wrong or have made a mistake.

11. I believe that things will fall into place.

12. I regularly look back on actions I have taken and think I could have done better.

13. I always wait for others to finish before I speak.

14. I often care more about how to do something best than why I am doing it.

15. I often feel that I am pulling more weight than others on my team.

16. I need to be held accountable or I may forget to do things.

17. I like when people need my help.

18. I listen to my gut.

19. I have a hard time saying no.

20. I would rather not do something at all if I can't do it perfectly.

Answer Key:

For each Mean Girl, you'll find the numbers that correspond to her behaviors and mindsets. Add up your responses for each group of numbers and see which Mean Girl has the highest score. If you find that two Mean Girls share a high score, consider how they interact with one another and dominate other traits.

The **Yes-Woman** is a people pleaser who puts everyone's needs above her own. (5, 7, 9, 13, 19)

The **Perfectionist** feels a need to be strong and do everything herself. (1, 4, 10, 12, 15)

The **Free Spirit** usually follows her gut feelings and intuition, and is often not comfortable with deadlines and structure. (2, 6, 11, 16, 18)

The **Achiever** can be overly structured, putting process over purpose, and feels life is an endless report card. (3, 8, 14, 17, 20)

Now that you know what kind of mean girl is sabotaging you, you can develop the tools to defeat her. She prevents you from being your best self not because her criticisms are accurate, but because they expertly prey on your deepest insecurities. Author Courtney E. Martin writes in her book, Perfect Girls, Starving Daughters[6], "We were taught we could be anything, but what we heard was we have to be everything." Once you realize that who you are already is exactly who you were meant to be, you can take the actions in the next chapter that will bring you closer to becoming your most badass self.

Passion

Chapter 4:
Your Personal Mission Statement

All organizations have mission statements, but some are better than others. Nordstrom's[z] mission statement is often touted as one of the best, for good reason:

"In our store or online, wherever new opportunities arise, Nordstrom works relentlessly to give customers the most compelling shopping experience possible. The one constant? John W. Nordstrom's founding philosophy: offer the customer the best possible service, selection, quality and value."

There is a famous story[8] of a customer walking into Nordstrom and stating that he wanted to return some tires. The clerk refunded him the money and the customer left, satisfied. The catch is, as many people know, that Nordstrom does not sell tires. This is an example of how Nordstrom lives its mission daily.

Even if you are not a multi-billion dollar company, your value as a person, an employee, and a colleague stems directly from how well you know your own values. Since you completed the values activity in Chapter 2, you are well on your way!

Fear is a powerful motivator. We stay in jobs for too long because we are afraid of looking like a "job hopper" or someone who can't figure out what they want. We compare ourselves to others and think that we're the only ones who haven't figured it out yet. We take opportunities that sound good on paper even when our gut says it's all smoke and mirrors. We take less money than we are worth because we are afraid to seem greedy, ungrateful, or like we're not a team player. We can be drawn in by excitement, opportunity for growth, and money. All of those are great perks but if we don't look inward and ask ourselves what gets us out of bed in the morning or what we want to hang our hats on professionally, we will end up right back in the place of discontent, wondering why this thing didn't fulfill us, either.

I once took a job that sounded perfect on paper - it was exactly what I had been looking for, the convergence of all the things I cared about in one place. I received an offer and replied with my counteroffer. The director said he would get back to me by Friday. By Sunday, I had not heard, and my heart sank. For me, this was a red flag. I don't work well in organizations where the person in charge routinely sets their own deadline and then fails to meet it without any explanation or interim contact. I did finally hear back from him at 11 pm on Sunday night. I weighed the counteroffer, the stated* mission of the organization, and my own desires. I ignored my gut concerns and accepted the job. It went on to be one of the worst years of my professional life. This person's tendency to overpromise and underdeliver showed up every day, in every way. It impacted every employee and every client. I had seen the signs that this would be the case before I ever accepted but I didn't listen to my own values because I wanted to believe it wouldn't impact me.

*The distinction of *stated* mission is very important here. To an outsider, the organization appeared to be fulfilling its mission. It can be very difficult to figure out how to identify alignment between stated mission and activities. Sometimes it has to be a leap of faith. Sometimes you can contact current or former employees, read publications or crowdsourced websites like Glassdoor.com, or talk to a current or former client. But even in the absence of any proof, my gut told me this wasn't right, and I ignored it.

In my experience, when people act emotionally or unprofessionally in the workplace, it's usually because they feel that a deeply held core value of theirs is being violated. When you can identify those values, like you did in Chapter 2, you can usually figure out why you're so upset and begin to identify solutions. But when an employee isn't attuned to their own personal core values, their emotions can overrun them and they often don't know why. One of the biggest mistakes we can make professionally is not knowing what our own *personal* mission statement is, regardless of the job we currently hold.

If you need some guidance, Idealist.com[9] published a post with the following simple formula to get you started on your own personal mission statement:

"To combine/synthesize/integrate/leverage (or similar verbs) my experience in _____ (a) with my interest in _____ (b) to _____ (c) for _____ (d)."

Using this formula, my personal mission is "to use my expertise in behavioral science and my advocacy skills to empower badass women to excel at what they do, stand tall, and own their value so they can light up the world." Give it a try and see what you discover about yourself!

Chapter 5:
What's Your Vision?

Reflect on the following questions. While you can simply think about your answers, I highly recommend you record your answers here or somewhere else. Not only does recording your answers allow you to be really concrete about them, but it can provide major insights in the future when you return to them.

What is your vision about the best possible outcome for the challenges you are facing now?

_____

_____

_____

If you were the best version of yourself, what would you be doing to address this situation?

_____

_____

_____

What would it mean for you to be successful in resolving this?

_____

_____

_____

What is it costing you to stay where you are, in terms of financial, time, energy, emotional, or relationship costs?

_____

_____

_____

What will achieving this change give you?

_____

_____

_____

How will you feel once you've solved your problems and achieved your goals?

_____

_____

_____

What is the first step you could take to move forward? Then what are the next steps?

_____

_____

_____

Is there any part of this challenge that is similar to one you have faced and overcome in the past?

_____

_____

_____

Does this situation reflect your core values? Where is there alignment and misalignment?

_____

_____

_____

What behaviors can you change *today* to impact this situation?

_____

_____

_____

What will help you stay accountable to yourself in following through as you work on this?

_____

_____

_____

What resources do you need to be successful?

_____

_____

_____

Finally, what is the functional benefit to staying where you are?

_____

_____

_____

Inaction is usually a result of a "good enough" status quo. For example, if you regularly feel under the weather, you may say that you want to find a cure for what ails you. But the "good enough" benefit to being sick is that you garner sympathy from others and have a reason to do things like stay home or reduce your workload at a job you hate. There is no shame in identifying the "good enough" reason for your stagnation, in fact, naming it will allow you to bring it into the light so you can examine it and make the necessary changes to start living your best life.

Chapter 6:
Having it All

Your life will never follow perfectly the carefully crafted plan you've laid out for it. You need to have a vision for the highest possible achievements, yes, and also contingency plans for when life inevitably throws you for a loop. Facebook COO and author of *Lean In* Sheryl Sandberg literally wrote the book on how to be a boss at work and then suffered a tragedy that shifted her entire life. As the first female director of policy planning at the State Department, Anne-Marie Slaughter was leading the definition of that Lean In life when her family needed her and she made a choice. These women are not failures. These are exactly the parts of life you need to anticipate and do your best to plan for in advance.

Cycle of Purpose Activity

For the following items, rate how strongly you agree with each statement on a scale of 1-10. You will use these ratings as guidance while you complete the Cycle of Purpose[10] that follows. This activity has been adapted from the book Co-Active Coaching[11] as a tool to assess your overall satisfaction with your life.

1. I can clearly articulate my value system.

2. I can clearly articulate my personal mission statement.

3. I have strong work/life balance.

4. I sleep at least 7-9 hours per night.

5. I wake up feeling well-rested.

6. I have time to exercise.

7. I have time for the activities I enjoy.

8. I have opportunities for quiet reflection.

9. I believe in the purpose of my place of employment.

10. I believe that my place of employment values me.

11. I make enough money.

12. I would support the choices I have made if I were looking from an external perspective.

13. I have a clear vision for my life.

14. I believe I can have it all.

15. I believe I am enough.

Consider the various domains of your life as components of a wheel. Each area you want to tend to falls between two spokes. List out every domain that matters to you. You can use the guide below, or you can use your own. For each domain, rate where you are currently on a scale of 1-10. If you feel that an area of your life is really strong, like you have a regular exercise practice that makes you feel powerful and healthy, mark it a 10 and put a dot at the outer limit of the wheel for "Health." If you have absolutely no time to date and see no change in that circumstance anytime soon, mark it a 1 and put a dot at the center of the wheel for "Romance." Once you have done this for every domain, connect each dot to make a circle. In a perfect world, you would mark every domain of your life as a 10 and be able to roll along your journey smoothly and without bumps.

But you don't live in perfection. Your cycle of purpose will never stay perfectly, permanently round. As soon as you get one area of your life under control, another will surprise you and get completely bent out of shape. You will never roll along smoothly on your journey of life without incident. It will bend unexpectedly, causing bumps and bruises, and make you feel at times that you are bouncing along a dusty, unpaved road. Once you let go of the expectation that this road will be smooth, you will be liberated from expectations of perfection. Your life, your career, and your personal relationships will all ebb and flow in intensity, satisfaction, and demand.

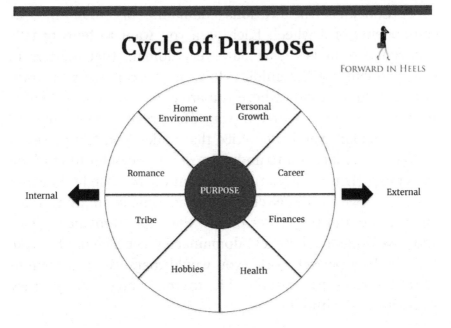

As you consider what insights you have gained from this activity, remember that there are different domains of your life. They are never going to be 10/10 across the board. That's not how life works. Perfection is not the goal. Nature abhors a vacuum and when one domain is "perfect" another will test you. The point is to have enough strategies in your toolbox to handle any bumps on your journey.

Potential

Chapter 7:
Getting in the Right Mindset to Kick Ass

Now that you have taken stock of where you are, how can you get yourself in the right headspace to make these major life changes? A mindset shift called reframing is a simple attitude change that will dramatically increase your quality of life.

Many of us are huge fans of hyperbole. Why tell someone you are hungry when you can tell them you are wasting away as we speak, punctuated by as many dramatically place expletives as possible, accompanied by a gif? While this approach might be amusing when deployed positively in a joking manner, it can also backfire in negative situations. Using that same mentality, a setback at work can become a career-ender, a holiday weight-gain can turn into berating yourself for lack of self-control, and an unexpected breakup can lead to an internal monologue about how unlovable you are.

Negative thinking is so pervasive in our culture that we often don't notice this running commentary in our heads, undermining our success. There are different kinds of ways to engage in negative self-talk. The most obvious is by directing harmful statements at ourselves. This includes looking in the mirror and saying, either out loud or in your head, something insulting. Some examples: "I look disgusting." "I'm so fat." "Nothing looks good on me, I might as well give up." Women are told constantly how far they are from attaining the moving target of perfection, to the point where even goddess/model

Chrissy Teigen is getting her armpit fat sucked out[12] to look better in dresses. No wonder we internalize those messages and direct them at ourselves.

The next kind of negative self-talk is deflecting compliments, lest we appear full of ourselves (aka confident). Rather than graciously saying "thank you," we scramble to find a way to delegitimize the statement. For example, we respond to "I love your jeans." with "They were on sale!" as if we are apologizing for having good taste and making up for it with a bargain. This kind of deflection isn't limited to our bodies or physical appearances, either. Women regularly preemptively apologize for having a thought or opinion, both verbally and in emails. This may not seem like negative self-talk, but how much less confident can you get than prefacing your contribution with a qualifier that says your thoughts really aren't that important?

The last common kind of negative self-talk is so subtle we usually miss it. It is the momentary gut reaction that says we are not good enough. How many times have we caught a glimpse of ourselves in a reflection from an unflattering angle, or without makeup, and thought, "Ugh, I look awful."? Or how many times have we ordered something to eat, silently judged ourselves while eating, and then felt sick and remorseful afterwards? There's no further commentary to it, no long diatribe toward ourselves and our choices, but that feeling in the pit of our stomachs does not vanish instantly. That pervasive feeling of self-judgment is probably the most insidious version of negative self-talk, because it feels like a mist we can never fully grasp. If asked how often we engage in negative self-talk, we would probably not even remember these moments, and if we are not aware of all the ways the habit can show up, it will be nearly impossible to <u>change it</u>.

So then, if it's everywhere, how DO we change this? We change this mindset with a technique called <u>positive reframing</u>. Positive reframing is not pretending everything is fine when it isn't, or stopping yourself from experiencing negative or painful thoughts and emotions. Instead, it is a strategy that allows us to name our feelings and then think about how to approach them from a different angle.

Start with a simple example. Have you ever declined plans, only to see your friends having fun on social media and immediately experiencing extreme FOMO? Positively reframing this experience would sound something like changing, "I'm such a loser for staying in when everyone else is out having a good time" to "I love that my friends are such extroverts while allowing me to have my introverted moments." Notice that it doesn't erase the negative feeling, nor does it designate any one choice as the correct one. Positive reframing looks at a situation and rather than assigning blame or judgment, simply makes observations about what has happened and what it might mean if it is used constructively for the future.

Start <u>breaking this habit</u> with a simple, 5-step strategy. Remember that this is not a one-and-done process but a shift in your perspective that will require ongoing monitoring and checking in.

1. First, stop and notice when you are having a negative conversation with yourself. Refer back to the examples

above to remember that not all negative self-talk is direct and verbal.

2. Identify what evidence supports this idea. For example, if you tell yourself that you are not qualified for a job you want, ask yourself "Do other people with my qualifications have similar positions in this or other industries? Do I have a passion for this work and a willingness to learn? Does the job description have truly non-negotiable requirements in it that I do not meet, or more general desires for the position that I know I could figure out?"

3. Start to identify patterns. Are there consistent situations you find yourself in, or behaviors in others, that set you off on criticizing yourself? These are your triggers. Spend time thinking about where these might come from. Perhaps you had a parent, sibling, friend, significant other, co-worker, or boss in the past who treated you a certain way and you felt powerless to respond, so you turned inward to try to regain a sense of control over the situation.

4. Change "I" to "You" in your negative statements. Rather than saying, "I am so lazy" when you skip the gym again, say "You are so lazy" and notice the difference in how it feels. You would never tell your best friend, "You look fat and awful" upon seeing her in an outfit, so why is it okay to do the same thing to yourself? Externalizing the criticism can make it sound as harsh as it is because it implies telling someone else you love that they are not good enough, which you would never do.

5. Practice positive reframing every time you notice yourself engaging in negative self-talk. It can show up in any situation, in a variety of statements. Here are some examples to help you start practicing:

    "I can't believe I ate the whole thing, I'm so disgusting. No wonder my pants don't fit." → "I ate the whole thing and don't feel so well now. I am not going to beat myself up over it but next time I am tempted, I'll remember this unpleasant feeling."

    "I haven't lost any weight, even though I've been exercising. If it's not even going to work, I might as well save the money on a gym membership and lie on my couch." → "I've been exercising because I value my body and want it to be strong and powerful, and to keep me healthy for a long time. Fitness is an investment in my future, even if I don't see immediate, aesthetic results."

    "I hate my job, I hate my co-workers, I hate everything. I don't want to adult anymore." → "Things are tough right now and I'm feeling pretty disconnected from work. I wonder if I can change anything about my job, my situation, or even my expectations, and start to feel better."

    "I got ghosted, again. Obviously, I'm worthless and no one will ever love me. I'm going to die alone." → "I've learned some lessons about what I do and don't want in a relationship, and every experience gets me closer to finding the right fit."

"I'm in so much debt. I'm so irresponsible. I'm never going to climb out of this hole so I might as well treat myself." - "This mountain of debt can feel insurmountable when I look at the whole thing, but there are probably small steps I could start taking to improve my situation in the long run."

Chapter 8:
Setting SMART Goals

SMART Goals[13], whose origins are commonly attributed to Peter Drucker's *Management by Objectives*, are a great way to set yourself up for success. They are called that both because they stand for an acronym, which we'll explore below, but also because using them to outline your goals is a brilliantly strategic way to ensure you actually reach them. There are different versions of SMART Goals where the letters correspond to different words, and the beauty of this technique is that it allows you to tailor your goals to your own needs and preferred language. Below, I will outline the most common definitions for each letter and in parentheses, you can find some additional suggestions to help tailor SMART Goals for yourself.

SMART Goals

Specific (simple, sensible, significant)

Measurable (meaningful, motivating)

Achievable (agreed, attainable)

Relevant (reasonable, realistic and resourced, results-based)

Time-bound (time-based, time limited, time/cost limited, timely, time-sensitive)

1. ### Specific

Without clear parameters, you won't know what exactly you're trying to achieve.

What is the goal?

Why does it matter?

2. ### Measurable

If you don't know where you're starting and you don't know what benchmarks will show if you are progressing, you will end up doing a variety of activities to reach some ambiguous end result.

How will I know when it is accomplished in concrete, observable terms?

3. ### Achievable

Your goal should be both realistic and ambitious: likely to actually happen but still enough of a stretch that you need to put focused effort into it. If you're not a little scared, you're probably not dreaming big enough.

Can I accomplish this goal?

How realistic is the goal, based on other limiting factors, such as money, time, and resources?

Can I actually control this outcome or is it dependent on others?

4. **Relevant**

This goal should both matter to you and connect to other goals.

Is it worthwhile?

Does this match other needs?

5. **Time-bound**

All goals need a deadline to ensure urgency and accountability. Without firm deadlines, everyday tasks can take priority over bigger goals.

When can I accomplish this?

How can I backwards plan from that date to set milestones to move me forward?

What can I accomplish today?

What can I accomplish in one week?

What can I accomplish in one month?

Chapter 9:
What Every Job Must Have (No Matter How Old You Are, How Senior the Job, or What Industry You're In)

When I work with professionals looking to make a job or career switch, the first thing I drill into them is this: You are not a beggar. An employer who wants you knows that you bring more to the table than they do. Sure, they have money, benefits, and resources, but you have a particular skill set, drive, and ability to learn that they need desperately. Never think of yourself as powerless in the job search. As soon as you think it, it becomes true. An interview is like dating - when you're inexperienced or young, you think "I hope they like me." When you gain more experience, you realize it's about hoping you are *both* mutually a good fit for each other. Eventually, you realize you have not only the power, but the obligation to yourself, to assess that fit up front.

The job-hunting system disproportionately benefits the employers who built it. Don't get stuck thinking about job titles and what already exists – let your mind reach for the biggest, grandest, craziest idea you can think of, and work backward from there to something realistic and meaningful for you.

Your perfect job must allow you to do the following:

1. Use the skills you already have.

2. Learn the skills you don't yet have but want.

3. Identify an organizational culture that aligns with your value system.

4. Build your strategic network.

5. Meet your financial goals.

I credit an amazing mentor of mine, <u>Adam Simon</u>, with opening my eyes to these needs. First, identify what you are great at. Spend at least 5 minutes free writing an answer to this question. Include jobs, hobbies, volunteering - anything you have spent time doing, enjoyed, and were at least marginally good at. Don't censor yourself. Think expansively; include anything and everything.

_____

_____

_____

Next, name 3 people you have worked with (closely or from a distance) whom you admire. What do they do that you respect? This might cover the actual job, the way they conduct themselves, or something else that sticks out to you. Their positions can be anywhere in the company, but try to choose people you have actually seen in action, rather than well-known people you admire but have never met.

_____

_____

_____

Chapter 9: What Every Job Must Have (No Matter How Old You Are, How Senior the Job, or What Industry You're In)

Now, refer back to what you identified as values from Chapter 2. When making decisions, what must remain true for you?

_____

_____

_____

Then, fill in the following table. Think big picture all the way down to how you want to spend your day-to-day.

Consider:

1.   What do you need out of a job? (need to have)

2.   What do you want out of a job? (nice to have)

	Need to Have	Nice to Have
Salary		
Benefits (consider health/dental insurance, tuition assistance/reimbursement, gym reimbursement, professional development opportunities)		

Culture (consider values alignment, happy hours, start-up "all hands on deck" feel, clearly defined individual responsibilities, hierarchies/matrixed relationships, overlapping teams)		
Location (consider commute length, type of building, individual offices/cubicles, shared space, standing desks, work from home options)		
Work Style (flexible hours, start on time/end on time schedules, type of office space)		

Now how do you get this dream job?

List 5 people in your strategic network you can reach out to and discuss your career and growth. Scour Facebook, LinkedIn, and any other loose connections[14] you may have. Your strategic network comprises people one step removed from your friends - acquaintances and colleagues. Think about your hobbies. Are you in a social sports/running club, professional network, karaoke league, or other group that connects you with people you may not otherwise encounter? Commit to finding out <u>who you know</u>[15] in your industry or desired industry. Do some research, ask if you can buy them coffee or a drink, and conduct a 15-minute <u>informational interview</u>[16].

1. _____

2. _____

3. _____

4. _____

5. _____

Now identify your bottom line minimum necessary <u>salary</u>. Calculate your expenses using a website like <u>Mint.com</u> or even a basic expense calculator in Excel. Know what number you absolutely cannot go below to survive. Now dream bigger. Think about vacations, hobbies, retirement savings, vehicles, experiences, clothing, shoes, and anything else you want. Factor those into your salary needs. Also consider the frustratingly true fact that even when women ask for raises on par with men, they <u>receive them less</u>[17]. Money is energy; it fuels our ability to do the work. So, remember that when an employer is interviewing you, it is because you have something they need, and act accordingly. You've got this!

Results

Chapter 10:
Creating Your Action Plan

For each objective that will help you reach your goal, complete the following activity:

Action Plan	
Vision: *Write your overarching vision for your life here.*	
Objectives: *What big action items do you need to check off your to-do list to make this vision a reality?*	
Deadline: *When do these objectives have to be achieved by?*	
Backwards Plan: *What daily or weekly steps need to be achieved to reach your big objectives? (Add in as many as necessary to achieve your goals)*	Due Date: *Write the date for completion next to each item to keep yourself accountable*
1.	
2.	
3.	
4.	

5.	
Potential Barriers: *What stands in the way of achieving your dreams?*	
Overcoming Barriers: *What options exist for you to leap over these possible roadblocks?*	

Chapter 11:
Negotiating – Because You're Worth It!

Whew! You must be fired up at this point after all the work you've put in so far! Now that you've figured out your own personal needs, how can you take this information to your workplace? You know what you want and what you're worth, but how do you actually get it? First, you need to be armed with statistics. Then, you need to know the best strategies to ask for what you need. Finally, build your army of other badass women seeking the same things. There is not only strength in numbers, but support, camaraderie, and insights to be gained.

Sallie Krawcheck, former CEO of Merrill Lynch Wealth Management (among other venerable institutions), launched Ellevest, a digital investment platform for women, and Ellevate Network, the global professional woman's network. In Ellevest's recently published guide, "Mind the Gap," she outlines how gender disparities in pay, opportunity, and promotion impact women over a lifetime.

Lean In and McKinsey & Company partner annually to create Women in the Workplace[18], a comprehensive study of the state of women in corporate America. One of the conclusions they reached was that for every 100 women promoted to manager, 130 men are promoted. According to an internal study by Hewlett-Packard, women typically raise their hands for a promotion when they're 100% ready, whereas men apply when they feel only 60% ready. Women hesitate because they view the job descriptions as strict rules. The men seem to understand the unwritten rule that there's some wiggle room where undeveloped potential can make up for missing qualifications.

Every year in April, the United States commemorates <u>Equal Pay Day</u>. This date symbolizes how far into the following year women must work to earn what men earned in the previous calendar year. The date is even later in the year for women of color and women with disabilities. The gender pay gap, as it's known, is the disparity between what women and men make for doing the same jobs. The estimate hovers around 80 cents (women) to the dollar (men) on average, with different sources putting it as low as 79 cents or as high as 82 cents (yay?). In other words, a 20-year-old female entering the workforce full time will lose $418,800 over a 40-year career compared to a male worker, which means she will have to stay in the workforce **10 years longer**[19] than a man in order <u>to earn the same amount</u>[20].

"Okay, okay, I get it, I know there's a problem. <u>What am I supposed to do about it</u>?"

I'm so glad you asked!

1. Do your homework on a website like <u>Glassdoor</u>, <u>Payscale</u>, or <u>Indeed</u>. Find out how your salary compares to the salaries of your peers, both male and female, not only in your company but across your industry. This preparation is key to making your case.

2. Detail all of your accomplishments and contributions to your workplace. Write down every

single thing you do that is above and beyond your current job description. Be exhaustive. Get testimonials from colleagues, even if you feel awkward asking. Tie all of the work you've done to results for the company's bottom line. It is not up to you to consider whether or not they have the money to give you what you're asking for. Men don't do that.

3. Find out what <u>protections</u> or <u>resources</u> might exist in your city or state.

4. Practice negotiating in your everyday life to become comfortable with it. Ask for your latté on the house, your credit card's annual fee to be waived, or a voucher for future travel from an airline that didn't meet your needs. Role-play with a friend as your boss. Really practice the delivery, and your poker face. You need to be confident and firm while not appearing rude or unyielding. Make statements and don't turn them into questions by letting your voice go up at the end or by engaging in <u>vocal fry</u>[21]. Most importantly, remove your personal feelings from the whole process. Think of it like selling a vacuum; you believe in the product (your work), you believe it's worth this price (your raise), and your job is to get your potential sale (your boss) to see it as worth that same price by rooting your pitch in what it can do for them.

5. Now it's time to make the <u>big ask</u>! Schedule a meeting (or maybe you have a performance or

annual review coming up) with your manager, lay out your case, and ask for a raise based on your worth. Ideally, let your manager propose the first concrete number. Have your dream number in mind, as well as the one you can comfortably live with and feel valued by. Counter with your dream number, and then WAIT. Silence is powerful and uncomfortable. Resist the urge to fill it. If they return with a number you are not comfortable with, stand your ground. You are not asking for a favor. You are valuing yourself and your work, and increasing your loyalty and productivity to a company that is willing to recognize you for it. No matter what they offer, even if it's what you want or higher, keep your poker face straight and say you would like some time to think it over and will get back to them once you've considered it.

If your company absolutely cannot or will not budge on money, you can ask for other perks. You can negotiate for more vacation time, a flexible schedule or location, a new title, a leadership coach, increased benefits, childcare options, and plenty more. Remember that it costs them so much more money[22] to recruit, hire, and train a new employee and have them get comfortable with culture and other intangibles than to give you what you are asking for. You can also ask for a performance-based review at a sooner interval, like 3 or 6 months instead of 12.

Ellevest published a "Mind the Gap"[23] Guide to help women negotiate, and one frustrating conclusion they found is that women who negotiate for a promotion or compensation increase are 30% more likely than men who negotiate to receive feedback that they are "bossy," "too aggressive," or "intimidating." However, women are more <u>likely to be granted a raise</u>[24] if they root their request in language that focuses on the company's overall success and show that they care about fostering positive relationships at work. While this might feel like playing the game and therefore not toppling the patriarchy, remember that by standing firm and demanding what you are worth, you are part of closing the gender pay gap. The patriarchy hates that kind of stuff.

Chapter 12:
Burnout Prevention Plan

Think back to your values exercise. Remember how long your journey was to get to your core values. Your life is a marathon, not a sprint, and if you're trying to run each individual mile at top speed, you're going to burn out long before you reach the finish line.

There are 168 hours in a week. Rather than focus on how much you can cram into one day, take a big step back and look at your whole life from a 30,000-foot view.

Answer the following big-picture questions:

What is your vision for your life?

_____

_____

_____

What is your personal mission statement?

_____

_____

_____

What are your biggest priorities?

_____

_____

_____

From here, think about the next year. Depending on your preferences, look 12 months forward from now, or if you prefer to anchor to the end of the calendar year or the change of a season, do that. Then zoom in a little more until you're down to the next month. Finally, take another look at your 168-hour week. Chances are, by this point, the tasks you thought you had to accomplish this week seem a lot less urgent than they did at first. This is because you started big and narrowed in, rather than focusing on what is immediately in front of you. By doing this, you told your brain that there is plenty of time, and allowed it to relax as it planned, instead of telling it that everything was priority #1.

A 2014 study by the social networking company The Draugiem Group found that the top 10% of employees[25] with the highest productivity didn't put in longer hours than anyone else, and often didn't even work full 8-hour days. Instead, the key to their productivity was that for every 52 minutes of focused work, they took a 17-minute break. In fact, there is a study dating back to the early 1980s that divided undergraduates into two groups: one group was advised to set monthly goals and study activities; the other group was told to plan activities and goals in day-to-day detail. The assumption was that the granular, structured agenda would lead to higher productivity, but in fact the opposite turned out to be true. Failing to plan for inevitable distractions or unexpected events meant that all of the time spent meticulously planning ended up actually being wasted time on work that had to be redone to account for the speed bumps.

I have to admit, I am really bothered by seeing posts on social media about "Sunday Scaries." Seeing people post about them starting from the second I wake up on Sunday morning makes me feel robbed of my weekend. If you find yourself in that situation more often than not, it's time take control of your life. In other words, if you don't like Mondays, change them.

Most of us think that we want to front-load our weeks and give ourselves light Fridays to ease into the weekend. That's sort of true. Below I'm going to explain the optimal way to design your week to truly "work smarter, not harder."

Start by thinking about your week more holistically[26]. Instead of 8-hour workdays (or 10 or 15...), think about your time as a 168-hour week. Identify what you have to do, what must get done right away, what can wait, what you are dreading, what you can postpone, what you can rearrange, and most importantly, who you can recruit to be on your team. Stephen Covey calls this identifying big rocks[27], but use whatever framework works for you.

Fridays should definitely focus on low-stress work like long-term planning, big-picture goal-setting, and relationship building and maintenance. Schedule blocks of time to check in on your long-term goals. Look at your monthly or quarterly benchmarks and assess your progress. Make a plan for how to tackle items the following week.

Once you have a vision for the upcoming week, spend Friday afternoon focused on human capital. Schedule lunch with a client, colleague, or mentor. Make phone calls to people you have been neglecting. Set calendar or <u>Boomerang (a Gmail service)</u> reminders to email connections you haven't touched base with in a while. People will go into their weekends feeling pleased at the individual attention and it will foster positive ongoing relationships.

When you come back to work Monday morning, you will have a plan laid out for you already. You don't have to spend Sunday night dreading the office, making mental plans of how to tackle your to-do list, or wondering if you forgot anything. Your Sunday won't be a pre-Monday stressfest, but a truly relaxing part of your weekend, as it was intended.

Use your weekend momentum to slide into Monday with high energy and consult your vision from Friday. Organize your week around goals, anything that has come up since your Friday planning session, and block off time to work.

Tuesdays and Wednesdays you are at peak productivity. Save your most challenging problems for those days. Treat work time as if it's sacred, just as you would a meeting with a superior. Put it on your calendar, assign specific tasks and outcomes to it, then put your head down and tackle it.

Thursday's energy begins to wane, so continue being productive in the morning and save the afternoon for larger meetings. People are mentally shifting into weekend mode by Thursday, so schedule a meeting where brainstorming and consensus building are necessary. People will be motivated to compromise and come to agreements to avoid going into their weekend plans with stress hanging over them.

By shifting your mindset around the structure of a workweek, you will find yourself more efficient, effective, and happier. But if you find you've done all of this to make your work life the most balanced, productive, and fruitful experience it can be, yet you are still unhappy, it might be time to consider making a bigger change. Now consider the following questions as follow up accountability to the big-picture questions you answered previously. By zeroing in on where you can make those changes, both big and small, you will already be on your way to creating the life you envision.

What are the major roadblocks that will stand in your way?

_____

_____

_____

What sustainability strategies can you employ to prevent burnout?

_____

_____

_____

How can you hold yourself accountable to this plan?

_____

_____

_____

How will you know if you are successful?

_____

_____

_____

Boldness

Chapter 13:
Tying it All Together

You're almost there! You are so close to designing and implementing your big life plan, but before you can do that, you need to check in with your own emotional intelligence and tie together everything you have learned so far.

Emotional intelligence[28] (also commonly known as EQ or emotional quotient) is the ability to identify and manage your own emotions and the emotions of others. It includes three skills:

1. Emotional awareness, including the ability to identify your own emotions and those of others;

2. The ability to harness emotions and apply them to tasks like thinking and problem solving;

3. The ability to manage emotions, including the ability to regulate your own emotions, and the ability to cheer up or calm down another person.

The good news is that most researchers believe it is not a fixed skill, but one that can be developed throughout a lifetime. Dr. Travis Bradberry argues[29] that, "Emotional intelligence...is a flexible set of skills that can be acquired and improved with practice. Although some people are naturally more emotionally intelligent than others, you can develop high emotional intelligence even if you aren't born with it."

Why should you care? Maybe you're highly driven, ambitious, and competent. Isn't that enough? No, unfortunately. Not only do all people benefit from being able to intuitively understand the experience of someone else, but women in particular have the added burden of being expected to have this skill automatically. Emotional intelligence is not the same as being nice, accommodating, or a doormat. It does not mean you have to start every sentence with "Sorry, …" or finish every thought with "But that's just my opinion." Rather, it means that you can read the verbal and nonverbal clues someone is giving you to their state of mind.

Dr. Bradberry finds in his book, <u>Emotional Intelligence 2.0</u>[30], found that "emotional intelligence is the strongest predictor of performance, explaining a full 58% of success in all types of jobs." Across everyone and every industry they studied, 90% of top performers were also high in emotional intelligence, while only 20% of bottom performers were. Further, people with high EQ make almost $30,000 more annually than those with low EQ.

<u>Psychology Today</u>[31] finds that "with high EI, you can succeed in many areas of your life. Your close relationships can benefit from knowing how to read people's feelings, regulate your own emotions (especially anger), and understand what you're feeling, and why.

"… leaders must have the ability to understand social interactions and solve the complex social problems that arise in the course of office life. From resolving disputes to negotiating high-powered deals, business leaders need to be able to read each other's signals, as well as understand their own strengths and weaknesses." Studies on this topic have become so common that Harvard Business Review[32] even has an option for you to follow all Emotional Intelligence tagged publications, and repeated publications show high correlations between EQ and success[33].

Author Ashley Zahabian[34] writes that "the best way to be more emotionally intelligent is to stop and question your feelings before you act. Think about why you really want something you're craving. Is it actually something that's good for you, or are you just giving into your immediate gratification addiction?" She goes on to argue that "every business is in the business of building people. If you cannot build people, you can't do anything. Building people requires delayed gratification...It requires regulating emotion and controlling behavior, because it is not easy to build somebody who is a little bit under you, because it takes patience, it takes self-management, it takes leadership."

How do you build these muscles, you ask? With another simple 5-step plan!

1. Stop and notice. Don't do anything with your observations yet. Simply become aware of your behaviors and thoughts, and identify if anything starts to resemble a pattern.

2. Observe your health habits. Are you getting enough sleep? Are you eating well or are there staples of your diet that send you into sugar highs and then crashes? Are you exercising in whatever way feels good to you? Are you regularly reading/watching/listening to news

or TV shows that stress you out or calm you? Do you meditate or otherwise take time for yourself during the day? Do you have strong friendships and relationships? All of these factors impact your ability to notice your own emotions and control them.

3. Take inventory of your work environment. Is your office a place you feel productive? frenzied? calm? Do you have colleagues that support you or compete with you?

4. Start to flesh out those patterns you were noticing earlier. Are there consistent behaviors in others that set you off, either in anger, sadness, worry, or some other negative emotion? These are your triggers. Spend time thinking about where these might come from. Perhaps you had a parent, sibling, friend, significant other, co-worker, or boss in the past who treated you a certain way and you felt powerless to respond, so you're reliving those patterns now.

5. Let go of your ego. Life is not a zero-sum game; you don't fail if someone else succeeds. In fact, women achieving success are much more likely to reach back and bring more women with them. What's good for one is good for all. Be able to ask yourself if you responded to a situation as the best version of yourself and if you could do better next time. Be able to hear feedback and criticism without feeling that your entire self-worth is being attacked.

Chapter 14:
Big Life Plan

Now that you have checked in with your core self and feel confident in your ability to assess both your own and others' emotional needs, it's time to set out and design that life you deserve. The idea of designing your life comes from two awesome Stanford professors[35] named Bill Burnett and Dave Evans who initially set out to help students figure out how to get the jobs they wanted post-graduation. Using their research and frameworks, I have tailored their work specifically to focus on the needs of badass women ready to excel at what they do, stand tall, and own their worth so they can light up the world!

The researchers emphasize that the best course of action is not to comprehensively research all data for the perfect solution but rather to explore each alternative all the way to completion, and then gauge potential satisfaction with each solution. To do this successfully requires collaboration with everyone on your journey. No perfect dream job exists out there, and if you believe you are chasing a unicorn you will set yourself up for failure. Rather, your best course of action is to design the closest thing to your dream job through an active process of creation, accepting that there will be some compromises and adjustments.

Design requires a lot of options and good alternatives, and the ability to make good choices and lean into them with confidence and without second-guessing or what-if-ing.

Start by letting go of "<u>sunk costs[36]</u>." These are costs that have already been paid and therefore can never be recovered. Although it's primarily used as a business term, there are many examples of sunk costs in everyday life. One example is when you go out to dinner on vacation and order too much food, then keep eating once you're full because you think, "I already paid for it, so I have to eat it." No one can eat that food after you, and you can't take it with you because you're not in your home to repurpose it as leftovers later. That cost has been sunk and you don't benefit any further by making yourself sick. Another example is thinking that you must stay in a particular job or industry because you already paid for a degree or spent a number of years learning the trade. That's in the past and you do not improve your investment by staying in a job you hate. One final example that is all too common is continuing to date someone you have spent months or years with simply because you have invested time and energy into improving your relationship already. If it's not working, it's not working. You can't get that time back or make it more worthwhile if you stay and hope for the best despite all evidence to the contrary.

Next, explore all of your options. Dream as big as you possibly can, not limiting yourself in any way. Sketch out in any way that feels comfortable for you (visually, in a spreadsheet, with manipulatives, etc.) how each of those pathways could go. Follow each path to its natural conclusion, even if you have dozens of sub-possibilities. This will probably look overwhelming at first, but stick with it.

Once you have all of your tree branches or "what-ifs" laid out, begin to narrow down the most interesting, likely, and fulfilling options. Edit or adjust if necessary. Once you feel confident in your ambitious yet feasible options, it's time to make a choice. Choose[37] what will make you happiest, most satisfied, and fulfill your needs in life. Once you've chosen, let go of the rest of the options. Don't think about them again. They are not unchosen options in a Choose Your Own Adventure[38] book; they are no longer viable options. Research[39] shows that there is such a thing as too much choice, and when there is, people are less satisfied with their selection.

Now, this isn't to say that you will definitely choose the right option for you on the first try. You might choose based on all of the best information you have at the moment, and end up finding out more information later that would have changed your perspective. Think back to the reframing your mindset activity in Chapter 7 and remember the strategies you learned to reduce your negative self-talk. You may initially feel like a failure when you reconsider your choices, but remember that these are all data points for you to make a better decision for yourself next time. Start by writing down the decision you considered to be the "failure" or "wrong choice" in the most objective terms you can. Then, identify the answers to the following growth insight opportunities: what can be learned, what went wrong, and what could be done differently in the future. Every time you make a decision that you later come to wish you had made differently, complete this exercise again, ideally in the same notebook, journal, or spreadsheet. You will begin to identify patterns that might be informing other choices in your life you'd like to change, as well.

Chapter 15:
Conclusion

You did it! Not only have you have reached the end of the book, but along the way you unearthed your own value system, learned how those values impact your professional and personal life, created strategies to ask for what you want and need, and designed your ideal life. You deserve a glass of wine, or at least a nap!

Remember, however, that this is an ongoing journey. In your lifetime, you will revisit these insights many times, and often you will find that they have shifted since the last time you checked in. There is no final outcome, no state of reaching happiness and perfection forever. My yoga instructor says, "Balance is the space between *effort* and *ease*." While she was talking about tree pose, I think it applies to life too. You can both celebrate when things are good, like your work, and acknowledge that it means by definition other areas are being neglected. No one will ever be able to be 100% present in every single area of their lives. The lifelong work is in constantly adjusting your balance and deciding where to dedicate more focus at one time vs. another. Remember there is a chasm between "I'm a bad person" and "I'm a person who did a thing I regret." We are all beautiful, imperfect, glorious works in progress.

That said, sometimes the big-picture perspective isn't as helpful when you're in the weeds, but it can help to remember that what you do today and today alone does not dictate your whole life. When it comes to eating, exercising, working, spending time with family, or any other domain of your life, you will never knock it out of the park every day in every way. What you can do is name it and adjust what's within your control. If you find you still need more help in figuring out the tools to help you succeed, ask for that help from friends, family, or professionals like a coach or therapist.

You have one final activity to complete now. Set aside some quiet time and write a letter to your future self. Attach a significant milestone to it, like "age 40" or "10 years from now" or "when I make partner" or "when I buy my home." Close your eyes and envision who you are on that day, then start writing. Here is an example of a letter I wrote to myself when I started on my journey to create Forward in Heels.

Dear Jenny,

Today is your 40th birthday. Congratulations on looking so youthful! You dedicated a lot of time and energy to protecting your skin, from staying out of the sun and wearing sunscreen to moisturizing to drinking lots of water and getting lots of sleep. Your hard work paid off in that area and many others. You completed graduate school while working full-time, took low-paying and stressful jobs to complete your requirements for clinical licensure, and worked multiple jobs so you could build Forward in Heels into the premiere coaching and therapy firm for badass women. To accomplish this, you had to learn what you didn't know, persevere when you hit stumbling blocks, regularly assess progress and adjust course if necessary, and invest your money wisely. You didn't always make the correct decision the first time, and you had to handle that when it happened.

You humbled yourself when you made mistakes and you asked for help, something that is not easy for you. You did all of this while maintaining your personal relationships, making sure that even while busy, you let those in your life know how important and valued they were to you. Sometimes this required putting aside a project for a moment to send a text and sometimes it required showing up in person. The payoff for this is that, time and again, those people have showed up for you when you needed them and kept your life well-rounded and fulfilling.

You have friends and family you love and you have designed your life on your terms. You travel, constantly experience new things, and still have a beautiful home to return to that is all yours in the city you love most. You are able to donate both time and money to charities that matter to you, using the comforts your life has achieved to continue to do good in the world. You are healthy and strong, and you constantly find ways to challenge yourself mentally and emotionally to continue to grow as a person.

You still have so many goals to pursue and you will achieve them using the same grit you've demonstrated so far. You are a badass who excels at what you do, stands tall, and owns your worth. Keep lighting up the world!

Love,

Jenny

FORWARD IN HEELS

Appendix

1. Frank and Ernest used with the permission of the Thaves and the Cartoonist Group. All rights reserved.

2. Carter, Sherrie Bourg, Psy.D. "The Tell Tale Signs of Burnout ... Do You Have Them?" *Psychology Today*. Posted Nov 26, 2013. https://www.psychologytoday.com/us/blog/high-octane-women/201311/the-tell-tale-signs-burnout-do-you-have-them

3. PBS.org. A Science Odyssey: People and Discoveries. *Abraham Maslow 1908 – 1970*. http://www.pbs.org/wgbh/aso/databank/entries/bhmasl.html. Image created by author.

4. Tegze, Jan, Senior Recruiting Manager at SolarWinds. "Reasons Why People Quit Jobs: What I Learned During Ten Years." Published on September 16, 2016. https://www.linkedin.com/pulse/reasons-why-people-quit-jobs-what-i-learned-during-ten-jan-tegze/

5. Hill, Patrick, and Turiano, Nicholas. *Journal of Research in Personality* as quoted in New York Magazine article "Living With Purpose Yields a Longer Life and Higher Income" by Drake Baer. Posted on January 4, 2017. https://www.thecut.com/2017/01/living-with-purpose-yields-a-longer-life-and-higher-income.html

6.   Martin, Courtney E., *Perfect Girls, Starving Daughters: The Frightening New Normalcy of Hating Your Body.* Simon & Schuster. 2007.

7.   Nordstrom Mission Statement from website, https://shop.nordstrom.com/c/company-history

8.   Mikkelson, David. "Nordstrom Tire Return." Published April 30, 2011. https://www.snopes.com/fact-check/return-to-spender/

9.   Goldberg, Amy-Louise. "Job search need some direction? Create a professional mission statement." May 13, 2014. https://idealistcareers.org/job-search-need-some-direction-create-a-professional-mission-statement/

10. Kimsey-House, Henry, Kimsey-House, Karen, Sandahl, Phillip. *Co-Active Coaching.* Nicholas Brealey. 2011. http://www.coactive.com/why-cti/buy-the-book

11. Kimsey-House, Henry, Kimsey-House, Karen, Sandahl, Phillip. *Co-Active Coaching.* Nicholas Brealey. 2011. http://www.coactive.com/why-cti/buy-the-book

12. Lebsack, Lexy, and Sasso, Samantha. "Chrissy Teigen Got Liposuction & Doesn't Care What You Think." Posted May 5, 2017.

http://www.refinery29.com/2017/05/153132/chrissy-teigen-liposuction-confession

13. "Management by Objectives." The Economist. The Economist Group Limited. Posted October 21, 2009. https://www.economist.com/node/14299761

14. Feloni, Richard. "Why Acquaintances Are More Valuable To Your Career Than Your Closest Friends." Posted December 4, 2014. http://www.businessinsider.com/career-value-of-weak-ties-2014-12

15. Bell, Elliott. "How to Ask for an Informational Interview (and Get a "Yes")." https://www.themuse.com/advice/how-to-ask-for-an-informational-interview-and-get-a-yes

16. Zhang, Lily. "3 Steps to a Perfect Informational Interview." https://www.themuse.com/advice/3-steps-to-a-perfect-informational-interview

17. Cohn, Laura. "Women Ask for Raises As Much As Men Do—But Get Them Less Often." September 6, 2016. http://fortune.com/2016/09/06/women-men-salary-negotiations/

18. Krivkovich, Alexis, Robinson, Kelsey, Starikova, Irina, Valentino, Rachel, and Yee, Lareina. "Women in the Workplace 2017." https://www.mckinsey.com/global-themes/gender-equality/women-in-the-workplace-2017

19. National Women's Law Center Fact Sheet. March 2017. https://nwlc.org/wp-content/uploads/2017/03/Women-and-the-Lifetime-Wage-Gap-2017-1.pdf

20. Vasel, Kathryn. "5 things to know about the gender pay gap." April 4, 2017. http://money.cnn.com/2017/04/04/pf/equal-pay-day-gender-pay-gap/

21. Dunn, Thom. "What is 'vocal fry,' and why doesn't anyone care when men talk like that?" July 28, 2015. https://www.upworthy.com/what-is-vocal-fry-and-why-doesnt-anyone-care-when-men-talk-like-that

22. Kantor, Julie. "High Turnover Costs Way More Than You Think." February 11, 2016. https://www.huffingtonpost.com/julie-kantor/high-turnover-costs-way-more-than-you-think_b_9197238.html

23. Ellevest. "Mind the Gap." http://production.assets.ellevest.com/documents/Ellevest-Mind-the-Gap-Guide.pdf

24. Bernard, Tara Siegel. May 14, 2010. "A Toolkit for Women Seeking a Raise." https://www.nytimes.com/2010/05/15/your-money/15money.html

25. Gifford, Julia. "The secret of the 10% most productive people? Breaking!" August 20, 2014. https://desktime.com/blog/17-52-ratio-most-productive-people/

26. Dahl, Melissa. "A Google Exec on How to Organize Your Workweek." December 15, 2015.

https://www.thecut.com/2015/12/google-exec-on-how-to-organize-your-workweek.html

27. Covey, Stephen. "7 Big Rocks."
    https://www.youtube.com/watch?v=fmV0gXpXwDU

28. "Emotional Intelligence." *Psychology Today.*
    https://www.psychologytoday.com/us/basics/emotional-intelligence

29. Bradberry, Travis Ph.D. "Why You Need Emotional Intelligence to Succeed in Business." January 21, 2015.

30. Bradberry, Travis Ph.D., and Greaves, Jean. *Emotional Intelligence 2.0.* TalentSmart. 2009.

31. Whitbourne, Susan Krauss, Ph.D. "Unlock Your Emotional Genius." February 2, 2013.
    https://www.psychologytoday.com/us/blog/fulfillment-any-age/201302/unlock-your-emotional-genius

32. Ovans, Andrea. "How Emotional Intelligence Became a Key Leadership Skill." April 28, 2015.
    https://hbr.org/2015/04/how-emotional-intelligence-became-a-key-leadership-skill

33. Deutschendorf, Harvey. "Why Emotionally Intelligent People Are More Successful." June 22, 2015.
    https://www.fastcompany.com/3047455/why-emotionally-intelligent-people-are-more-successful

34. Ashley Zahabian   Quote from/link to forbes.com article   34

35. Designing Your Life. https://designingyour.life/blog-home-page/

36. "Sunk Cost." https://www.investopedia.com/terms/s/sunkcost.asp

37. Objective Insights Decision Analysis v2. https://www.objectiveinsights.com/wp-content/uploads/2015/10/Objective-Insights-Decision-Analysis.pdf

38. Choose Your Own Adventure book series. https://www.cyoa.com/

39. Schwartz, Barry. "More Isn't Always Better." Harvard Business Review, June 2006. https://hbr.org/2006/06/more-isnt-always-better

Made in the
USA
Middletown, DE